Cheryl
MILLER

CHERYL MILLER
Basketball Hall of Famer
& Broadcaster

by Brian Howell

ABDO
Publishing Company

Published by ABDO Publishing Company, PO Box 398166, Minneapolis, MN 55439. Copyright © 2014 by Abdo Consulting Group, Inc. International copyrights reserved in all countries. No part of this book may be reproduced in any form without written permission from the publisher. SportsZone™ is a trademark and logo of ABDO Publishing Company.

Printed in the United States of America,
North Mankato, Minnesota
102013
012014

 THIS BOOK CONTAINS AT LEAST 10% RECYCLED MATERIALS.

Editor: Holly Saari
Series Designer: Christa Schneider

Library of Congress Control Number: 2013946590

Cataloging-in-Publication Data

Howell, Brian, 1974-
 Cheryl Miller: basketball Hall of Famer & broadcaster / Brian Howell.
  p. cm. -- (Legendary athletes)
Includes bibliographical references and index.
ISBN 978-1-62403-131-1
1. Miller, Cheryl, 1964- --Juvenile literature. 2. Women basketball players--United States--Biography--Juvenile literature. 3. African American women basketball players--United States--Biography--Juvenile literature. 1. Title.
796.323/092--dc23
[B]

                                                    2013946590

TABLE OF CONTENTS

Cheryl Miller was the star of the talented girls' basketball team at Riverside Polytechnic High School in California.

105 Points

Nearly every time forward Cheryl Miller touched the ball on the night of January 26, 1982, it found its way into the net. It did not matter whether she used her right hand or her left, shot jumpers or layups. Miller seemingly could not miss.

Miller was a senior at Riverside Polytechnic High School in California. The Riverside Poly Bears had one of the best girls' basketball teams in the entire country, with Miller leading the way. Of all the great games Miller and Riverside Poly played, it was that night in 1982 that fans remember best.

Miller was already considered the best high school girls' basketball player in the country. She would go on to have one of the most remarkable careers in the history of the sport. She was an All-American in high school and an All-American and national champion in college. She won an Olympic gold medal, coached at the college and professional levels, and then became a broadcaster for the sport. She has been inducted into several basketball halls of fame.

Topping 100

On that night in 1982, Riverside Poly faced the overmatched Braves of Norte Vista High School. The Norte Vista team did not have many experienced basketball players—certainly not anybody who could stop Miller. With the help of her teammates, who were very talented as well, Miller scored a national-record 105 points in the Bears' 179–15 win. At the time, only one girls' basketball player had ever scored 100 points in a traditional five-versus-five game. As of 2013, it had been accomplished just twice more.

For Miller to get her 105 points, the 6-foot-2 forward had a nearly perfect night. She attempted 50 field goals

Record-Breaking Game

For Riverside Poly, the game on January 26, 1982, went into the record book. The Bears' 179 points was still a national single-game record for a high school girls' basketball team through 2013. The 84 points they scored in the first half was a national record at the time. It lasted all of one half, as the Bears scored 95 points in the second half. That record has been broken several times since, but the 84- and 95-point halves were still among the top 10 in history through 2013.

and made 46. She also shot 15 free throws and made 13. "I hit my first six jumpers," she said. "I was laying it up with my left hand, which I never do. Everything I tossed up was going in."[1] She even dunked the ball once. It was the first-known time a woman had ever dunked a basketball during a game.

Before that night, Miller's best game was a 77-point effort the year before, also against Norte Vista. Scoring even 77 points is a remarkable accomplishment. Through 2013, it still ranked among the top-10 individual scoring performances in national high school history. That night in 1982, Miller blew past her previous mark before the fourth quarter.

Performance of a Lifetime

The crowd realized Miller was about to make history.

Quite a Night

On the night Miller scored 105 points against Norte Vista High School, her younger brother Reggie Miller had a great night too. Reggie, who was playing for Riverside Poly's boys' basketball team, scored 39 points against Norte Vista's boys' team. On most nights, it would have been considered a great night for Reggie. Cheryl stole the spotlight that night, however.

They chanted for her to reach 100. Miller did not pay attention to the crowd though. She simply focused on playing the game. "Through all of that surround-sound, I could hear my heart beating," she said. "It was a stillness . . . a calm. It's this whole chemical and physical transformation where it's just you. The ball felt like a part of my hand and the game was in slow motion."[2]

Miller finally came out of the game for good with three minutes to play. She was so focused on playing well, she had no idea how many points she scored. A fan at the game actually told her the news. "He said,

100-point Scorers

Reaching 100 points in a single game is a rare feat in basketball. Wilt Chamberlain is the only player to have reached that mark in the National Basketball Association (NBA). He scored exactly 100 points on March 2, 1962.

The 100-point mark has been reached fewer than 10 times in a college game and fewer than 25 times in a high school game. Just four players in history have scored 100 points in a high school girls' game while playing the standard five-on-five rules:

- 113—Epiphanny Prince, Murry Bergtraum (NY), Feb. 2, 2006
- 105—Cheryl Miller, Riverside Poly (CA), Jan. 26, 1982
- 101—Lisa Leslie, Morningside (CA), Feb. 9, 1990
- 100—Linda Page, Dobbins Tech (PA), Feb. 15, 1981

In addition, several players scored 100 points in Iowa when that state played six-on-six basketball. Because the rules of that game were so different, those records are not included in the national books.

'Dude, you scored 105 points!' I was like, 'What?'" Miller said.[3] Everyone in attendance was amazed at how incredible Miller was that night. "For a girl to grab the ball like that . . . it was just unbelievable to watch her. She was a woman among the girls," said Dale Roberts, a former administrator at Riverside Poly.[4]

Criticism of the Game

There were some who felt that beating a team by 164 points showed poor sportsmanship. Riverside Poly coach Floyd Evans said the Bears tried to keep the score down. They had called off the full-court press early in the game and went into a zone defense, which would allow Norte Vista to slow the pace of the game. Nevertheless, Miller and her teammates kept scoring and scoring.

Special Moments

Epiphanny Prince broke Miller's single-game high school scoring record in 2006 with 113 points for Murry Bergtraum High School in New York. Much like when Miller had her big night, Prince and her coach were criticized for embarrassing the other team. Miller defended both of their remarkable performances. "That's what the game is all about, special moments in special situations," Miller said. "Instead of people getting their feelings hurt, they should pat [Prince] on the back."[5]

But Braves head coach T. J. Bienias did not have anything negative to say about Miller. He simply said she was remarkable. And when the game was over, Norte Vista players asked Miller for her autograph. "This was her opportunity to do something she may only do once in a lifetime," Bienias said. "She came up to me after the game and thanked me for letting her do that. She did it on her own. We kept trying to stop her."[6]

Miller was tough to stop—not just on that night but throughout her career. Following high school, Miller would go on to a remarkable career in college, with Team USA in the Olympic Games, as a coach, and as a broadcaster. However, it would be tough to match that night in 1982. "It was probably my single greatest game," she said.[7]

Miller went on to win an Olympic gold medal with Team USA.

CHAPTER 2

Saul Miller, *left*, was always supportive of his daughter's
athletic pursuits.

Childhood

Standing 6 feet 5 inches tall, Saul Miller had the height and talent to excel on the basketball court. In the 1940s, Saul was a star at Hamilton High School, an all–African American school in Memphis, Tennessee. Following his great high school career, Saul went to LeMoyne College (now LeMoyne-Owen College) in Memphis and was a star there too. He even earned all-conference honors.

Saul was also an exceptional musician with a talent for playing jazz on the saxophone. He played with jazz legends such as B. B. King and John Coltrane. Saul also played the sax for the Phineas Newborn quartet. In 1955, Saul invited a young nurse, Carrie Turner, to come see him play in the Phineas Newborn quartet at the Flamingo in Memphis. During a break, Saul and Carrie danced.

An Athletic Family

Not long after that date, Saul and Carrie, who also played basketball in her youth, got married.

Saul then re-enlisted in the US Air Force so he could financially support his family. He was a computer systems superintendent, and Carrie was a registered nurse. In 1963, Saul was transferred to March Air Force base, located in California's Riverside County. The young family—Saul and Carrie had two sons by then—settled in Riverside, California.

Not long after, on January 3, 1964, Cheryl Dean Miller was born. She was the third of five children for Saul and Carrie, and she gave her parents an immediate scare. Cheryl was born with her breath cut off by the umbilical cord, which was wrapped around her neck. It was only a temporary scare, however, and Cheryl soon proved to be a remarkable little girl. "You love them

An Environment for Success

Saul and Carrie Miller raised their five children to become successful adults. There were tough times, of course, but a lot of good moments too. Saul used his background in the air force to establish discipline in the home. Carrie worked hard as a nurse, but she always made sure her kids had a hot meal. Carrie's oatmeal became a regular part of the morning in the Miller household.

"One thing I remember my father always telling all of us is that there's a seed of greatness in all of us and that it was up to him and my mom to provide a healthy environment," Cheryl said during her Naismith Memorial Basketball Hall of Fame speech in 1995. "But, ultimately it was up to us to cultivate, to nurture that seed. It was my responsibility to make it grow. [Mom and dad], you raised me, and the four other kids, to be the very best that we could possibly be."[1]

all, all the same, but Cheryl just shined," Carrie said.[2]

All five of the Miller children—Saul Jr., Darrell, Cheryl, Reggie, and Tammy— displayed great athletic talent in their youth. Saul Jr. was considered a great athlete, but he focused on the saxophone rather than sports. Darrell played professional baseball from 1979 to 1990, including five seasons in the major leagues with the California Angels. Reggie played for 18 seasons with the Indiana Pacers of the NBA, retiring in 2005. Tammy displayed her talent in volleyball. She earned a scholarship and played at California State University, Fullerton.

Tough Cheryl

It was evident very early in Cheryl's life that she would be an athlete. She did not care for

Reggie Stars on the Court

Like his older sister, Reggie Miller became a star on the basketball court. In 1987, he was the eleventh overall pick of the NBA Draft, selected by the Indiana Pacers. For 18 years, Reggie was a star shooting guard for the Pacers. He averaged 18.2 points per game for his career. He also connected on 2,560 three-pointers, which ranked second in NBA history as of 2013. In 2012, he was inducted into the Naismith Memorial Basketball Hall of Fame.

the things girls often like. "I ripped the frilly stuff off all my dolls," Cheryl said. "I gave Barbie a butch cut. I brutalized Raggedy Ann."[3] Influenced by her athletic parents and older brothers, Cheryl preferred sports and being active. "Growing up, I thought I was the only girl who sweated," she said.[4]

She sweated, all right. She also bled and took more than her fair share of lumps. Her older brothers did not take it easy on her. Cheryl might have been their little sister, but they made sure she got tough. "They'd trip me, make me skid on my knees and then laugh," Cheryl said. She continued:

> They'd throw me a ball, tackle me, pile me, mangle me . . . But they were real proud of me being able to throw and kick balls and fight and stuff. I did everything I could to make them happy. I got so tough I was queen of John Adams grade school.[5]

Queen of the Court

She was the queen of the Miller court too. Saul built a half court in the backyard, and the kids learned the game on that court. Cheryl started playing basketball at around five years old, learning many of the fundamentals from her father. She took elbows going against Saul Jr. and Darrell, and it made her better.

One day, at age nine, she went out to the court and began draining shots. From inside the house, Saul took notice, and he walked outside. "He said, 'There's something special about you, Cheryl.' Then he went back in," Cheryl said. "That was it."[6]

Although she also played her older brothers on the court, Cheryl really connected with Reggie. Separated by less than 20 months, Cheryl and Reggie grew very close. "Reg and I are close. Like this," Cheryl once said, making a fist with her hand.[7] They also played together on the backyard court that Saul constructed. They helped each other become great players, even at a young age. In fact, they got so good that they started playing others for money. "Back in the fifth and sixth grades, we'd go to the courts at John Adams Elementary or Hunt Park and hustle two-on-two games,"

Beating the Boys

At age 10, Cheryl played on a fifth-grade boys' basketball team, and she was dominant even then. "The boys on the other teams laughed at me in the beginning, but then they'd see the score at the end of the game and they weren't laughing anymore," she said.[8]

"Cheryl, a lot of people wish they could be in the house with the greatest of anything. I just so happened to live across the hall from absolutely, positively the greatest women's basketball player ever. I'm proud to say I am not on this stage if it wasn't for you, Cheryl Dean. We as a Miller family would not be held at a high level if it wasn't for you. We rode your shoulders all the way here, so thank you very much."[10]

—Reggie Miller, during his Naismith Memorial Basketball Hall of Fame induction speech on September 7, 2012

Reggie wrote in his 1995 book, *I Love Being the Enemy.* "We had it down to a science. It was the best hustle scam in Riverside, California."[9] Cheryl pretended she did not know how to play basketball. Then she and Reggie would usually crush their opponents on the court.

Cheryl's childhood set her up for basketball stardom. Her parents gave her the discipline and support she needed. Her siblings made her tough and gave her challenges. It was clear to everyone who knew her, though, that Cheryl was just getting started.

Cheryl started playing basketball at a young age and quickly improved.

Cheryl Miller was an all-around player with many skills on the court, including ballhandling.

High School Days

With Saul and Carrie Miller's own histories of playing sports, it was no surprise they had athletic children. It was also no surprise Saul and Carrie did all they could to help their children succeed.

Saul was especially influential for his children when it came to athletics. "Their father was responsible for their being athletes," said Tim Mead, who worked in the front office of Major League Baseball's California Angels. "He's really been their coach as well as their father. Whichever sport they decided to concentrate on, he concentrated on it too. If Cheryl needed to practice her hook shot, he'd be out there watching her."[1] That dedication helped Darrell Miller get to the majors with the California Angels (now Anaheim Angels), and it helped Reggie Miller get to the NBA. Saul's dedication also helped Cheryl become one of the best girls' basketball players in the country by the time she was a freshman in high school.

Dominating All Four Years

When Cheryl got to high school in the fall of 1978, state-sanctioned girls' sports were still fairly new. Riverside Polytechnic High School, located in the Southern Section of the California Interscholastic Federation (CIF), began crowning section champions in 1974. Before Cheryl arrived, the Riverside Poly Bears had never won a section championship. In fact, as of 2013, the Bears had not won one since she graduated, either. But during her four seasons at Riverside Poly, the Bears were dominant.

Cheryl's freshman year did not get off to a good start. She broke her ankle before the season. Then she sprained it during the season. When she did that, she felt like Saul might be disappointed, so she apologized.

Dr. Dad

During Cheryl's freshman year of high school, she hurt her ankle a couple times. The doctor suggested she tape her ankles before playing. Saul took it upon himself to learn how to do it and started taping Cheryl's ankles before she got on the court.

"Cheryl had never been taped before," Saul said. "Our doctor told us that if she opened her eyes and even looked at a ball, she was to be taped. A relative was visiting who was studying sports medicine at the University of Arkansas. I told him I wanted to learn the right way to do it. Pretty soon I was taping the whole team."[2]

He was not disappointed, though, and fortunately Cheryl's ankle was just fine.

A sore ankle was about the only thing that went wrong for Cheryl as a freshman. Just 15 years old, Cheryl was already 6 feet tall, and she dominated on the court. That season, she scored 25.1 points per game and led the Bears to a 24–3 record and their first CIF Southern Section title. Performances by Cheryl and senior guard Marsha Overton helped the Bears defeat Alta Loma 54–44 in the section championship game. Overton was named Southern Section player of the year that season— the only year Cheryl did not receive the award.

As a sophomore in 1979–80, Cheryl took her game to a new level. At 6 feet 2 inches tall, she was easily the best player in the Southern Section. She averaged 30.5 points per game and was

Making History

During her high school career, Cheryl scored on slam dunks twice—in separate games against Norte Vista. At the time Miller graduated from high school in 1982, she was believed to be the only female to have ever dunked a basketball during a game. "When I dunk, it's like I'm on Cloud 15," she said. "But I can't do it every time out. I don't have it down pat yet. The conditions have to be just right, the game situation, the condition on the floor. But I know I can do it if my timing is right."[3]

named the Southern Section player of the year. Led by Cheryl and junior Meg Gallagher, Riverside Poly went 28–1 and rolled past Long Beach Poly 64–48 in the section finals.

Cheryl was more dynamic than ever before as a junior in 1980–81. She averaged 39.4 points and 16.3 rebounds per game. Because nobody could stop her, she took a lot of shots near the basket. That helped her make 75 percent of her shots that season.

During a game against the Norte Vista Braves that season, Cheryl scored 77 points. At the time, that was the second-highest single-game total for girls' basketball in national high school history. A pair of seniors, Gallagher and Sara Lewis, and junior guard Renee Overton also played exceptionally well that season. It was Cheryl who stole the spotlight, however, driving the Bears to a third straight section championship.

Cheryl completed her high school career with a brilliant senior season in 1981–82. Posting 37 points per game, Cheryl led Riverside Poly to yet another undefeated season and another section championship. For the first time, Riverside Poly also played for a state championship, which had been created only the year before. In that game, the Bears defeated Los Gatos High School 77–44. Cheryl scored 41 points—a California

Both Cheryl and her brother Reggie went on to play Division I
college basketball.

record for a state tournament game—while also posting
16 rebounds, 7 steals, and 4 blocks.

The Team Star

Riverside Poly was the most impressive team in
the state, possibly the country, during those four
years. Cheryl certainly did not do it alone. The Overton
sisters (Marsha and Renee), Gallagher, and others also
performed well. Renee Overton, in fact, set a national

record (which has since been broken) for most assists in a single game with 32 on the night Cheryl scored 105 points against Norte Vista in 1982.

Though Cheryl had great teammates, there was no question she was the brightest star of them all. "That was a little unusual team," Saul said of Cheryl's team her senior year. "They didn't just depend on [Cheryl]. But by playing with someone like her, they were so much better."[4]

Saul taught his daughter to be an all-around player, and she certainly was that for the Bears. "We considered it a privilege to coach people like [Miller]," Riverside coach Floyd Evans said years later.[5] For her career, Cheryl scored 3,446 points (33.8 per game), pulled down 1,564 rebounds (15.3 per game), and handed out 433 assists (4.2 per game). During her senior year,

"[Cheryl] never thought about herself first. She worked just as hard as we did and spent a lot of time outside of practices developing her game. She gave everything. Her work ethic and intensity was tremendous."[6]

—*Meg (Gallagher) Sanders, high school teammate of Cheryl and, as of 2013, a member of the Arizona State University coaching staff*

Cheryl grabbed 672 rebounds, a national record at the time. During her career with the Bears, the team went 132–4 overall. At one point, they won 84 consecutive games.

National Attention

Cheryl was not just a star in California; she had become a national star. She was the first high school basketball player—male or female—to be named All-American by *Parade Magazine* four years in a row. Although still in high school during the winter of 1981–82, Cheryl was already being touted as one of the all-time great players in the women's game. "You know what Lew Alcindor did for men's basketball? Well, that's what Cheryl Miller is going to do for women's basketball," Judy Holland, a former coach at the University of California, Los Angeles

Recruiting

There were approximately 250 colleges around the country that pursued Cheryl in hopes that she would play for them. Between letters and phone calls, the Millers were seemingly in constant contact with college recruiters. In order to let Cheryl concentrate on playing, Saul handled most of the recruiting process. "All he was doing was making sure that no one took advantage of me," Cheryl said.[7]

(UCLA), said during Cheryl's senior season at Riverside Poly. "I think she'll revolutionize women's basketball. Wherever she goes, that school is going to be ranked."[8]

At the end of her senior season, Cheryl had not yet decided where she would play college ball. She did not know by the time she graduated high school either. Those in the basketball community spent the summer of 1982 waiting to find out where the most dominant player in the game would end up.

Cheryl, *right*, was a strong defensive player.

CHAPTER 4

Cheryl Miller playing for USC in February 1983

College Hoops

Throughout the summer of 1982, Miller kept college coaches around the country on edge. She was the number one high school recruit in the country, but unlike other top recruits, Miller still had not decided where to play in college. She did narrow her choices to hometown schools University of Southern California (USC) and UCLA, as well as national powers University of Kansas, Louisiana Tech University, and University of Tennessee.

Finally, on August 12, 1982, less than four weeks before the fall semester, Miller announced she would stay close to her Riverside home and play for USC. "Cheryl is the difference between USC being in the top 10 and being the top team," said UCLA coach Billie Moore, one of several coaches to heavily recruit Miller. "Her skills at this stage are probably further along than those of any other player to come out of high school."[1]

a leap forward in the standings. "We were competitive [without Miller]," Sharp said. "But when we'd go up against teams like Tennessee and Louisiana Tech, we always seemed to be one player short. But now we have Cheryl. She's the finest triple-threat player I've ever seen."[2]

Paula McGee was already a star at USC, having led the Trojans in scoring the previous year. She recognized right away that Miller was a dynamic addition to the team. "She can do it all," McGee said. "She has an eagerness to get going, to see what college basketball is all about. She wants to see if she's the Cheryl Miller she thinks she is, or perhaps the player other people think she is."[3]

Miller's college career was barely under way in the fall of 1982, yet she was already being talked about as possibly the best player in the history of women's basketball. *Sports Illustrated* ran an article about her that fall with the headline "She May Well Be the Best Ever."[4] That article was published after Miller's first game in a Trojans uniform. But Miller was humble. "I don't consider myself a superstar," Miller said at the time.[5] Miller might not have considered herself a superstar, but almost everybody else did—and throughout her career with the Trojans, she certainly gave them reason.

Successful First Season

It did not take long for Miller to establish herself as an invaluable contributor to her team and one of the finest players in the college game. She scored just 11 points in her collegiate debut, a 105–62 rout of Pepperdine University, but she made a statement soon after. Facing Northwestern University on November 30, 1982, USC rolled to a 110–80 win. Miller scored 39 points, a school record at the time. She made 16 of her 22 shots that night and added 8 steals and 6 assists. USC went on a 13-game win streak to open Miller's freshman season. That included a 64–58 win against two-time defending national champion Louisiana Tech, breaking Tech's 59-game win streak.

During her freshman year, Miller led the Trojans in scoring, with 20.4 points per game, and in steals, with 3.5 per game. She also averaged 9.7 rebounds and 3.5 assists, propelling her toward her first collegiate All-American honor.

In late January 1983, the Trojans lost back-to-back games—including a rematch with Louisiana Tech. Those were the only two losses the Trojans would suffer all season, going on to win their final 18 games. During the national semifinals on April 1 in Norfolk, Virginia, Miller led USC to an 81–57 rout of the University of Georgia. Miller scored 16 points and grabbed 14 rebounds in that game. Two nights later, the Trojans

Miller, *center*, celebrates after her USC team won the 1983 NCAA championship game.

once again met up with Louisiana Tech. USC won this time, 69–67, to claim its first national championship. Miller scored 27 points, a championship-game record. She was 11-for-14 from the free throw line and added nine rebounds, four blocks, and four steals to earn tournament Most Valuable Player (MVP) honors.

Better Sophomore Year

As good as Miller was during her freshman season, she would only get better. During Miller's sophomore season in 1983–84, she averaged 22.0 points and 10.6 rebounds per game. Because of this, she was awarded the most prestigious honor in college women's basketball: the James Naismith Award, which honors the best player in the nation.

That season, the Trojans started 10–0 before a three-game losing streak. They went 19–1 the rest of the way, though, finishing 29–4 and going on to win another national championship. This time, the Trojans defeated Louisiana Tech in the Final Four before knocking off Tennessee 72–61 in the finals. Miller scored 16 points in the

Grammy Appearance

As a sophomore at USC in February 1984, Miller made a brief appearance on television during the Grammy Awards, which annually recognize outstanding musicians. During the show, five-time Grammy Award-winner Donna Summer performed her hit song, "She Works Hard for the Money." As Summer performed, Miller came from offstage and dunked a ball through a hoop. "I've never been so nervous," Miller said at the time. "I was afraid the ball would bounce off my foot and hit Michael Jackson or somebody in the audience."[6]

While in college, Miller played for Team USA in the 1983 Pan American Games.

championship game and was named tournament MVP for the second year in a row.

Final Seasons at USC

Paula and Pamela McGee both graduated after that season, leaving two big holes in the USC lineup. Still, Miller's game was as good as ever. In fact, those were her two best seasons, statistically.

As a junior in 1984–85, Miller averaged career highs in points (26.8 per game) and rebounds (15.8 per game). She also posted 3.9 steals per game. Once again, she won the Naismith Award as college basketball's top player. That season, she had a remarkable performance with 36 points and 20 rebounds to lead USC to an upset of the second-ranked University of Texas Longhorns. Later in the season, she had 43 points and 23 rebounds in a close loss to Louisiana Tech. Three times that season, Miller broke USC's single-game scoring record. She also set a school record for rebounds in a single game with 24. "Women's basketball is Cheryl Miller," said former Louisiana Tech player Kim Mulkey, who later became a national coach of the year at Baylor.[7] But Miller was unable to lead her team to a third-straight championship. USC lost in the second round of the NCAA Tournament.

During her senior year, 1985–86, Miller posted an average of 25.4 points, 12.2 rebounds, and a career-best 4.0 steals per game. USC went 31–5 during that season and advanced to the national championship game for the third time in her four years. Miller and the Trojans could not close her career on a high note, however. Texas rolled past USC 97–81 to complete an undefeated season. Miller had 16 points that night, but none in the second half, and she fouled out of the game with 7:30 left to play. Still, she earned another Naismith Award that year.

Legendary Figures

Miller was the brightest star at USC from 1982–1986, but she was not the only one. Cynthia Cooper was a two-time national champ at USC. Cooper later helped the United States win a gold medal at the 1988 Olympics and bronze at the 1992 Olympics. In 2011, she was voted one of the top 15 players in Women's National Basketball Association (WNBA) history, having led the Houston Comets to four league titles and earning two MVP awards. She was named USC's head coach on April 11, 2013.

Pamela McGee was a two-time champion and first-team All-American at USC. She helped the United States win a gold medal at the 1984 Olympics. After winning two national titles and becoming a two-time All-American at USC, Paula McGee, Pamela's sister, played professionally for a few years, mostly in Europe.

Rhonda Windham was an all-conference player at USC. She became the first African-American general manager in the WNBA, holding that position for the Los Angeles Sparks.

Record-Setting Career

It was not the best way for Miller to end her career, but it was a career that few players in the history of the game can match. She is still the only women's player through 2013 to win the Naismith Award three times. She won other national player of the year awards too. She was a three-time conference player of the year and a four-time All-American.

As of 2013, Miller still held USC's school records for career points (3,018), scoring average (23.6 per game), rebounds (1,534), rebounding average (12.0 per game), and steals (462). She was number two in career blocks with 320—one behind Lisa Leslie.

In her four seasons, Miller guided the Trojans to a 112–20 record, leading the team in scoring and steals all four

Education First

Saul Miller could tell early on that his oldest daughter would be a star in basketball. He also knew she could not depend on basketball for a career. Because of that, he made sure she focused on her studies in the classroom in addition to taking care of business on the court. "Your basketball will get you into college," Saul told his daughter. "[College sports] will use you to sell tickets. You have to use it to get educated."[8] Miller earned a degree in communications at USC.

seasons. She also led the Trojans in rebounding her last three years and in assists during her sophomore year. Miller owns each of the three top single-season scoring marks in USC history and both of the top single-season rebounding marks. She's the only player in Trojans history to record at least 100 steals in a season. In 2006, USC retired Miller's No. 31 jersey in a ceremony honoring one of the greatest athletes in the school's history.

Miller played during a time when women's basketball was rarely televised. Yet, she still served as an inspiration to younger players and an example for youth coaches to use in their teaching. Carol Callan, who has served as national team director for USA Basketball for years, was a coach at Fairview High School in Boulder, Colorado, during Miller's career at USC. "The first recognition I had of Cheryl was when she was at USC and they had won those two national championships in a row," Callan said. "[As a coach] you always were looking for things to use to motivate your own players and show, 'Here's what you can become.'"[9]

Miller rebounds during a March 1986 game while playing for USC.

CHAPTER 5

Cheryl Miller goes up for a shot during the 1984 Olympic Games in Los Angeles.

Team USA

Miller never shied away from the spotlight. Instead, she embraced it. No stage was too big for her. Miller dominated the high school courts in southern California. She also dominated the college courts while at USC. Whenever she put on a Team USA uniform and took on the world, the results were the same.

One of the first times Miller suited up for the United States came in 1982. Shortly after she graduated from high school, she went on a 23-game international tour with the US national team. Although the only high school player on the US roster, Miller averaged 16 points per game during the summer tour. She scored 16 points during a 54–53 win against the powerful Soviet Union team. "I was scared, I was tight, and I didn't want to make any mistakes against the Russians," Miller said. She continued:

But when the shots were there, I knew enough to take them. Looking back, I think that game, more than any other, helped me mature as a player. I know I had a lot less fear about making it at the college level after that expcrience. [1]

Miller always had a way of getting herself and her teammates loose. Before a game against Bulgaria during that 1982 summer tour, she and some of her teammates practiced fancy layups to warm up. "So, one time I went down the middle with the ball and slam-dunked," she said. [2] Whether it was dunking in pregame warm-ups or filling the stat sheet in meaningful games, Miller was often the brightest star on the court during international games.

Another Hall for Miller

Miller was included in the 2010 class of inductees for the International Basketball Federation (FIBA) Hall of Fame. As the most dominant player on a team that won an Olympic gold medal and a world championship, Miller is in select company. As of 2013, just 28 players had been inducted into the FIBA Hall of Fame.

Olympic Gold

But her best moment for Team USA came in 1984. That year, Los Angeles hosted the summer Olympics. It was just the third time that women's basketball was included in the Olympics—and just the second time the United States was a part of the event.

At 20 years old, Miller was one of the youngest players on the US roster. Her age was not much of a factor, however, considering eight of the 12 players were 22 years old or younger. Center Carol Menken-Schaudt was the only player older than 25. The young roster was full of talent, including Miller's USC teammate Pamela McGee. Despite nine future Women's Basketball Hall of Famers on the roster, Miller rose to the top and dominated.

Team USA opened with an 83–55 win against Yugoslavia. Miller scored 23 points to lead the way. She added 20 points in an 81–47 rout of Australia in

Star-Studded Lineup

Team USA's roster for the 1984 Olympics was loaded with great players. As of 2013, 9 of the 12 players on the roster had been inducted into the Women's Basketball Hall of Fame. Five of those teammates are also enshrined in the Naismith Memorial Basketball Hall of Fame. Women's Basketball Hall of Famers from the 1984 team include Denise Curry, Anne Donovan, Teresa Edwards, Janice Lawrence, Pamela McGee, Cheryl Miller, Kim Mulkey, Cindy Noble, and Lynette Woodard. Curry, Edwards, Miller, and Woodard are members of both halls of fame.

the second game and helped the United States roll past Korea, China, and Canada.

In the gold-medal game, Miller had 16 points, 11 rebounds, and 5 assists to help Team USA to an 85–55 win over South Korea. That completed a perfect 6–0 tournament for the United States. None of the games were close. Team USA won by an average of 32.7 points per game, with the opener against Yugoslavia, a 28-point victory, being the closest.

During the six-game Olympic tournament, Miller led Team USA in scoring (16.5 points per game) and rebounds (7.0 per game). She made 66.1 percent of her shots from the floor and 75.8 percent of her free throws. "Right now, I've achieved my ultimate goal,"

Defending Champs a No-Show

Political hostility in the 1980s spilled over into athletics. The United States led a boycott of the 1980 Olympics in Moscow in protest of the Soviet Union's invasion of Afghanistan. In response, the Soviet Union led a boycott of the 1984 Olympics in Los Angeles. The Soviet Union and other Communist countries declined to participate in the Games.

In women's basketball, the 1984 boycott took the two-time defending Olympic champion team from the Soviet Union out of competition. The Soviets took gold in the 1976 Olympics, going 5–0, including a 112–77 rout of Team USA. In 1980, the Soviets rolled to the gold again, easing past Bulgaria 104–73 in the championship game.

The Soviet Union team (which later became the Russian team after the dissolution of the Soviet Union in 1991) has won four women's medals in basketball since, three bronze and one gold.

Miller tries to get past a double-team during the 1984 Olympics.

Miller said after the gold-medal game.[3]

Other Team USA Victories

Miller's only opportunity to play in the Olympics came in 1984, but she wore the United States jersey on other occasions too. In 1983, following her freshman year at USC, a 19-year-old Miller led the United States to the FIBA World Championship in São Paulo, Brazil. The World Championship is the biggest international basketball tournament outside of the Olympics. The United States had won the previous world title in 1979 but settled for silver this time. Team USA went 6–2 during the tournament, losing twice to the Soviet Union by only three points total. Miller averaged 17.6 points, 4.4 rebounds, and 3.8 steals per game.

USA Dominates Hoops

In 1984, Team USA won the Olympic gold medal in women's basketball for the first time. Since then, the United States has dominated. From 1984 to 2012, the United States won gold in seven of the eight Olympic Games. The only exception was in 1992, when the Unified Team (a collection of former Soviet republics) won gold and Team USA settled for bronze. In Olympic history, Team USA is 58–3 in women's basketball, with two losses in 1976 and one in 1992. Through 2012, Team USA had won 41 consecutive games at the Olympics.

Miller shoots a layup while playing Korea in the 1984 Olympics.

Three years later, in 1986, Miller and Team USA went to Moscow to try to reclaim the gold at the FIBA World Championship. The United States and the Soviet Union were the top two teams in the world—and they played like it. Both went 6–0 to earn a trip to the gold-medal game. In the finals, Miller had 24 points and 15 rebounds, leading Team USA to a 108–88 victory. It capped yet another great tournament for Miller, who posted averages of 18.0 points and 7.9 rebounds per game.

Aside from the Olympics and World Championship, Miller helped the United States win gold medals at the 1983 Pan American Games in Caracas, Venezuela, and the 1986 Goodwill Games held in Moscow. But it was the 1984 Olympics that made Miller a star around the United States, leading to magazine articles, television interviews, and some guest appearances on televisions shows.

Miller reacts after winning the gold medal at the 1984 Olympics.

When Cheryl Miller graduated college, women's basketball players had few options to continue playing basketball.

Nowhere to Play

When Miller graduated from USC in 1986, few opportunities were available to women's basketball players after college. The WNBA, which has increased the popularity of professional women's basketball in the United States and proven to be a viable option for players after college, would not exist for another 11 years. The WNBA was not the first women's professional league, but it has been the longest lasting and most stable league in the United States.

When Miller was a freshman in high school, the Women's Professional Basketball League came into existence, but that league folded before Miller graduated from Riverside Poly. In 1984, while Miller was in the middle of her college career, the Women's American Basketball Association (WABA) launched. The WABA had hoped to keep up the momentum from Team USA's victory in the 1984 Olympics. But the WABA folded after one season, with some of the teams not even making it

through the year. Other leagues, such as the Women's
Professional Basketball Association, Liberty Basketball
Association, and the Women's World Basketball
Association, came and went quickly. Some of them
never played a game.

Possibility of Going Pro

At the time Miller graduated, the National
Women's Basketball Association (NWBA) was trying to
get off the ground. On June 5, 1986, the NWBA made
Miller the first choice of its college draft and assigned
her to the California Stars. Getting drafted by the
NWBA then was not as big a deal as getting drafted
by the WNBA is today. The WNBA Draft is televised,
and draftees and others are in attendance when their

The WNBA

Over the years, several women's basketball leagues have tried and failed to stick around. The WNBA was different because it had the backing of the top men's league in the world, the NBA. Carol Callan, national team director for Team USA, said the NBA used the 1995–96 women's national team as a test to see if women's basketball could sell. "What the marketers found out is yes, women's basketball will sell," Callan said.

"It made it a sticking point then for [NBA commissioner] David Stern to sell it to his owners. That was the beginning of the WNBA."[1]

Since the WNBA's inception in 1997, the majority of its teams have been based in NBA cities and played in NBA arenas. As of 2013, the WNBA had 12 teams, with the Los Angeles Sparks, New York Liberty, and Phoenix Mercury being original members.

Today, top women's basketball college players can continue on and play in the WNBA and professional leagues in other countries.

"Just because we're women, we don't work or struggle or compete or want to win any less than men. I always feel like a gunfighter and everyone is after me. We can be friends later. On the court I'm going to take you to the hole and stuff your mug. I'm thinking nothing but net at my end and you'll be lucky to get a shot off me at yours. I'll be in your mug all night and if you can be intimidated, I'll take advantage of that, too."[2]

—*Cheryl Miller*

names are called. When Miller was selected by the NWBA, the draft was not a big event, and it certainly was not on television.

Miller's public relations representative simply stated that Miller was looking forward to playing for Team USA at the Goodwill Games—stating no definitive plans beyond that. It is a good thing Miller did not plan on a career in the NWBA. Despite plans for a 48-game schedule and eight teams in the league, the NWBA never played a game.

Miller was offered a chance to play professionally in Europe. The Harlem Globetrotters, an exhibition team founded in 1926 that traveled the country to put on shows, asked her to play for them. She declined both offers.

With opportunities so limited and unstable, Miller never played professionally.

Miller with Harlem Globetrotters players in 2010

Considering the greatness she displayed at every other
level, it seemed unfortunate that Miller never got a
great chance to play as a pro. "In her sport, Cheryl was
as good as Michael Jordan," her brother Darrell said.[3]
Jordan made millions of dollars as one of the greatest
players in the history of men's basketball.

Playing Career Comes to an End

Miller's future changed in 1987. While playing
in a pickup game at USC, she was tripped by another

Greatest Women's College Player

The argument for the greatest college women's basketball player of all time often starts with two players: Miller and Brittney Griner. Griner played for Baylor University from 2009 to 2013. Miller had two national titles, earned three Naismith Awards, and averaged 23.7 points per game. The 6-foot-8 Griner won a single national title, two Naismith Awards, and averaged 22.2 points per game. Miller outshines Griner in rebounds per game, 12.1 to Griner's 8.8; assists per game, 3.9 to 1.6; and steals per game, 3.2 to 0.5. But Griner's team record, 135–15, beats Miller's 112–20. Griner also leads in 5.1 blocks per game, compared with Miller's 2.5, and has a field goal percentage of .569, just edging out Miller's .565.

player and suffered a serious injury to her right knee. Miller went to her parents' home in Riverside to start the recovery process. Despite the long road to recovery ahead, Miller was not ready to give up playing the game. She spent a year rehabilitating her knee in hopes of playing for Team USA at the 1988 Olympics in Seoul, South Korea.

In August 1988, shortly before the Olympics began, Miller went to Colorado Springs, Colorado, to participate in Team USA tryouts. She clearly was not the same player she was before the injury. She then re-injured her knee during tryouts. Miller was released from the team. "I am very disappointed about being released from the team, but sometimes the mind says one thing and the body says another," Miller said.[4]

Brittney Griner, who ranks with Miller as one of the best college women's basketball players in history, has gone on to play in the WNBA.

Opportunities Abound

Every year, dozens of women's basketball players finish their college careers and then embark on a professional career. Some get the opportunity to play in the WNBA, while others spend time playing in European leagues. Some players have been known to do both in the same year. "I think the women are very happy with the fact that the WNBA is there and they can still go overseas and still make more money," Miller said.[6]

Miller essentially disappeared as a player after that—until she decided to try out for the 1992 Olympic team. Although most had not seen her play since 1988, Miller gave it a shot. She was named one of 18 finalists for the team (12 were selected), but more knee trouble forced her to give up her spot.

Miller did not have a glamorous ending to her playing career, but she did not disappear either. Those around her knew that, with or without professional basketball, Miller was going to do just fine after college. "She could have a career in sports broadcasting, in communications," agent Ed Hookstratten said at the time Miller was finishing her career at USC. "She's young, she speaks well on her feet. She has grace—because of that, she'll go far."[5]

Those close to Miller were confident that she could be successful in other roles, such as a broadcaster or a coach, after her playing days.

After a successful playing career, coaching was a natural step for Cheryl Miller.

Coach Miller

Although her playing days were behind her, Miller did not lose her competitive fire. She just found a different way to fuel it. In 1987, she returned to USC to take a job as an assistant coach for her former head coach, Linda Sharp. Miller was on the USC coaching staff for four years: two with Sharp as head coach and two with Marianne Stanley. Miller left USC after the 1991 season. When she was not coaching at USC, Miller spent time working on her broadcasting career. She was on air for both ABC Sports and ESPN.

Top Coaching Job

In 1993, USC came calling again. This time, Miller's alma mater wanted her to take over as the Trojans' head coach. Stanley was being replaced over contract issues. She believed she should get the same salary as the men's basketball coach and was ousted after a lawsuit. Miller accepted the job. "I can't believe I'm back home," she said during a

Emotional Miller

Known as an emotional athlete during her playing days at USC and for Team USA, Miller did not lighten up as a coach. Some observers felt she was too emotional on the sidelines. But Miller simply stayed true to her personality. "The fact that they said I could do anything on the basketball court [as a player], that's not necessarily true. The only thing I couldn't control was my temper," she said.[3]

news conference to announce her hiring. "It's an awesome opportunity and an awesome responsibility, but I'm ready to go."[1]

Miller understood right away that the job was not going to be easy. She was back home, but it did not feel like it. She was not embraced with open arms when she started the job. In fact, many felt she should have been more supportive of Stanley and her efforts to achieve equal pay. A few USC players threatened to quit the team. At Miller's first meeting with the team, freshman Cindy Page asked Miller, "Don't you feel you've betrayed women's basketball?"[2]

Despite the controversy, Miller and assistant coach Fred Williams went about their work. "I told [the players] I want to be successful, and I can't help

Head coaching was a new adventure Miller was excited to embark upon.

Miller's Coaching Record

Miller had several successful seasons during her tenure as coach on the collegiate and professional levels. Her overall record as a college coach was 44–14, with her teams going to the NCAA Tournament in both seasons:

- 1993–94: 26–4
- 1994–95: 18–10

Her overall record for her four years coaching in the WNBA was 70–52, with her team making the WNBA playoffs in 1997, 1998, and 2000, and advancing to the WNBA Finals in 1998:

- 1997: 16–12
- 1998: 19–11
- 1999: 15–17
- 2000: 20–12

but be successful," Miller said. She continued:

If they have a problem with me, Fred and I will take students from the business school and make a team out of them. I wasn't entirely prepared for that first meeting [with the team], but I was prepared not to take any lip.[4]

Dealing with the controversy about her hire was not the only obstacle Miller had to overcome. She had never been a head coach before, and some questioned whether or not she could do the job. "That was one of the biggest issues, as far as evaluating her acceptance," said senior forward Lisa Leslie.[5]

Led by Leslie, already a two-time All-American, USC had one of the better teams in the country. Miller was able to get the Trojans to play like one of the best. USC won its first six games and stood 17–1 at one point in the season. The Trojans

Miller was known for getting heated on the sidelines.

"Cheryl Miller is an icon in the world of women's basketball. Our organization owes a lot to Cheryl for guiding us these first four years in this historic movement in women's sports. She has been influential in creating an identity for the Mercury and for all of that we are thankful. It is going to be a difficult task to replace her."[6]

—*Bryan Colangelo, president of the Phoenix Mercury, after Miller resigned as head coach in 2000*

finished the regular season ranked number seven by the Associated Press. They advanced to the Elite Eight of the NCAA Tournament. In that round, Miller and the Trojans were knocked out by Louisiana Tech, 75–66.

Overall, the Trojans went 26–4 in Miller's debut season. Without Leslie, who won the Naismith Award in 1994 before graduating, the Trojans slipped a bit during the 1994–95 season. They finished 18–10 and got to the NCAA Tournament again but lost to the University of Memphis in the first round. Still, with a 44–14 record in two seasons, Miller certainly seemed to be laying the foundation for a long, successful career as USC's head coach.

On to Other Opportunities

However, just six months after the loss to Memphis, Miller abruptly ended her tenure as head coach. She surprised just about everybody, and angered some, when she resigned out of the blue. "I've had a once-in-a-lifetime opportunity presented to me, one that was very difficult to pass up," she said at the time.[7] Four days later, Turner Sports announced that Miller was being hired as a reporter and analyst for its NBA broadcasts.

Despite success and enjoying her work in television, Miller was lured away from broadcasting just two years later. This time, Miller was hired as the first coach and general manager of the Phoenix Mercury—a charter member of the WNBA. She was the first coach hired by any team in the new league. "What a great

Tough Time Replacing Miller

When Miller resigned as head coach of the WNBA's Phoenix Mercury in 2000, the team had to go looking for a replacement. The Mercury hired one of Miller's USC teammates and WNBA legend Cynthia Cooper. Halfway through her second season with the Mercury, Cooper also resigned. She was replaced by Linda Sharp, who coached both Miller and Cooper at USC. Sharp finished the 2002 season in Phoenix before moving on.

Cooper and Sharp had a tough time matching Miller's success in Phoenix, going a combined 24–40 during the 2001 and 2002 seasons. In fact, in the six seasons after Miller left the Mercury, the team went through six different coaches and missed the playoffs every year.

hire," Carol Callan, national team director for Team USA, later said. She went on:

> Part of it is, when you're a WNBA team, it's a business and you've got to sell tickets. She was able to generate a lot of ticket sales and they were one of the top two teams early on in terms of ticket sales.[8]

In addition to generating ticket sales, Miller produced wins. She guided the Mercury to the playoffs in three of her four seasons, including a trip to the WNBA Finals in 1998. Throughout her time in Phoenix, Miller was popular with fans because of her animated style of coaching. She would bump shoulders with players. She was tagged with more technical fouls than most other coaches in the league. There were times she would even dance on the court with the team's dance team. It was a blow to the team, then, when she announced her resignation in 2000:

> This is an extremely difficult and emotional decision for me. I am the type of person who has to give 100 percent of myself, physically and emotionally, to each task I take on. And the grind of basically working 12 months a year for the last four seasons has taken a serious physical and emotional toll on me.[9]

After leaving the Mercury, Miller put her full energy back into another of her earlier passions: broadcasting.

Miller resigned as Mercury coach after four seasons.

CHAPTER 8

Cheryl Miller has had a successful broadcasting career.

Miller on Television

More than a decade after she last coached a game, Miller has the opportunity to hang out on the sidelines. Working for Turner Network Television (TNT), Miller has been the sideline reporter for TNT's NBA Thursday night coverage. "I love it," she said. "The coaching, huh-uh. The coaching will kill you. This is like a walk in the park. It's even better when you have two accommodating [teams]. I've had a terrific ride."[1]

Planning for a Career in Broadcasting

As a player, Miller had very few peers, if any. She certainly held her own as a coach too. Miller is just as comfortable behind a microphone and in front of cameras. "How many women can become sideline reporters in the NBA, ask the tough questions, not be intimidated at all?" asked Carol Callan, national team director for Team USA. "She was the first and probably only. She was a legitimate basketball player who had the personality to get on TV."[2]

Miller certainly is not the only former athlete to jump into broadcasting. There are thousands of sporting events broadcast on television every year, and many of them—from football to tennis, baseball to figure skating—feature former athletes providing commentary or analysis. But Miller stands out in the crowd.

Miller had always planned on a career in broadcasting, long before sports television became as big as it is now. As a senior in high school, she realized there were few opportunities to play professionally. "Unless another women's professional basketball league is formed before I graduate from college, my basketball career may end when I graduate from college," she said back then. "I want

Broadcasting Led Miller to USC

There were approximately 250 schools that recruited Miller to play basketball out of high school. USC head coach Linda Sharp knew exactly how to get Miller to play for her. "I wanted to study broadcasting, everyone knew that," Miller said. "Coach Sharp said it all: 'There are two good schools for broadcast journalism in the United States, Columbia and USC. Columbia doesn't have a women's basketball team.' That about wrapped it up."[3]

to go into communications, telecasting, I guess."[4]

Shortly after she tore up her right knee in 1987, Miller embarked on her broadcasting career. She was hired by ABC and ESPN. In her early days on television, Miller worked as a reporter on ABC's Wide World of Sports. She also worked as a sideline reporter during the 1987 Little League World Series and during the 1988 Olympic Winter Games in Calgary, Alberta. In addition, she was able to work on some of the network's college basketball coverage. Miller joined Turner Sports in 1995, leaving her job as USC's head coach to join TNT's coverage of the NBA.

Broadcasting Talent

Even as she stepped into WNBA coaching, Miller never fully gave up working in television. That actually caused

Career Preparation

Attending USC gave Miller a good opportunity to prepare for a career in front of the camera. USC was never shy about getting publicity for its players, especially during the years Miller played, because the team was so good. Under the direction of USC's sports information department, Miller learned how to dress for interviews and how to respond to reporters' questions. She was interviewed hundreds of times during her time at USC.

Miller interviewing LeBron James in 2006

outsiders to question her commitment to coaching.
While she coached the WNBA's Phoenix Mercury, she
would spend part of her offseason helping TNT on its
NBA coverage.

In 1998, the NBA had labor issues that cut the
1998–99 season short and got it off to a late start. It
also caused the season to end late, conflicting with the
Mercury's preseason schedule. Miller was criticized
for skipping some of the Mercury's preseason to focus
some energy on her television work.

Miller insists she gave her all to coaching, but she has always had a love for broadcasting. Since leaving the Mercury in 2000, she has been able to devote her time to that love. To succeed as a player and as a coach, Miller devoted countless hours to practice and preparation. Taking time to prepare has helped her succeed as a broadcaster too. She said:

> For me, it's a whole week's preparation. It's watching the games Monday through Wednesday, talking to players and coaches and everything. It's like coaching or scouting. You're reading newspapers, gathering information to find out who's injured, looking at trade scenarios to see who's bluffing and who's looking. . . . With broadcasting, if you feel that you have all the information you need, it's just going out there and having fun.[5]

Working with Reggie

Cheryl's younger brother, Reggie Miller, retired from the NBA in 2005. Two years later, the Boston Celtics tried to lure him out of retirement. But after trying to get his body in shape for a few weeks, Reggie declined Boston's offer.

Cheryl was pleased with Reggie's decision. The two of them have worked together at TNT since Reggie retired. Reggie worked as an analyst during games— sometimes the same games in which Cheryl was working on the sidelines. While the two have always been friendly rivals, they enjoy working together. "I can't tell him that, but it's great," Cheryl said. "I love it. I'm glad he didn't go back to Boston; I'm glad that he retired, and I see him . . . a lot more."[6]

The preparation and knowledge Miller brings to broadcasting is, in part, what has made her so successful in the role.

Cheryl stands with her brother Reggie Miller in 2005, after his last NBA game.

CHAPTER 9

Cheryl Miller's passion for basketball continues in her broadcasting work.

Ongoing Legacy

The history of women's basketball has produced some amazing players and legendary figures. Nera White was a brilliant shooter in the 1950s and 1960s, earning All-America honors 15 times on the Amateur Athletic Union circuit. Nancy Lieberman was one of the first great stars, both in college and internationally. Ann Meyers Drysdale, who starred collegiately at UCLA, became the first high school player to make the US national team and was the first female to sign a contract with an NBA team.

Lisa Leslie was a two-time Naismith Award winner in college, a four-time Olympic gold medalist, and a three-time WNBA MVP. Cynthia Cooper, Anne Donovan, Teresa Edwards, Rebecca Lobo, Candace Parker, Dawn Staley, Sheryl Swoopes, and Lynette Woodard are all in the conversation too. Most recently, Diana Taurasi, Maya Moore, and Brittney Griner have been game-changing players in their own right.

Miller's Impact on the Game

Still, very few players can claim to have had as much overall impact on the game as Miller. With a dynamic game and a charismatic personality, she became, perhaps, the first true superstar in women's basketball—a player who gained national recognition from all types of sports fans. "You look at the growth and development of women's basketball, where it was and where it is today, women's basketball needed personalities," said Carol Callan, national team director for Team USA. "There were great players along the way, but Cheryl was probably the first player to take women's basketball to [the] media that was looking for names to hook on to."[1]

On the court, Miller was a unique player. She was a 6-foot-2 forward who could do

Confident Millers

Cheryl and Reggie Miller were both known to have some attitude on the basketball court. There was a reason for that. "A lot of people look at my brother Reggie and myself and think that we are cocky and arrogant, and maybe we are but only in the sense that we believe in ourselves and our talent," Cheryl said.[2]

Miller, *left*, and Lisa Leslie had their USC jersey numbers retired in 2006.

Miller's coaching skill helped bring the Phoenix Mercury to the playoffs in three of the four seasons she coached the team.

it all: score, pass, rebound, steal, and block. She is often credited for being the first player to take the women's game "above the rim," meaning that she did not just rely on jump shots or layups. She could dunk the ball.

Not everybody liked the way Miller played. Some followers of the sport were turned off by her showmanship. She was known to put up a shot and keep her bent wrist high in the air as she backpedaled down the court—a sign of arrogance that she knew her shot was going in. She did cartwheels on the court. She would point at the scoreboard and laugh. She would taunt the opponents and blow kisses to the crowd. Miller was unique, and while that didn't appeal to everybody, she remained true to who she was. "I have never been an act," she said. "I'm always spontaneous. I'm impatient and hyper and emotional and it

Guest Star

With her career as a broadcaster, Miller has certainly proven to be comfortable in front of television cameras. In addition to her work as a broadcaster, she has been a guest star on several television shows over the years, including the drama *Cagney and Lacey,* sitcoms *Living Single* and *Hangin' with Mr. Cooper,* and Nickelodeon's *Sports Theater.*

Miller has interviewed many NBA superstars, including Kobe Bryant.

all comes out on the court."[3] Count Lieberman among the legends who appreciated what Miller did for the game of women's basketball. "Of course Cheryl has revolutionized the game," Lieberman said as Miller was wrapping up her college career. She continued:

> She's taught young girls to play hard all the time and to be physical. She learned to do that the same way I did—we had to play like the guys. The flamboyance is her bread and butter. She sees those cameras and she seizes the moment. Sure, it's all Hollywood, but that's OK, too. I think Cheryl is the best thing that could have happened to the game.[4]

Callan said she has seen and personally known so many great players over the years that it is difficult for her to pinpoint the greatest player of all time. She credits Miller, however, for changing how forwards play the game. Until Miller, players her size played with their backs to the basket. "With a player like Cheryl," Callan said, "if you need to they can dribble the ball up the court. They give you so many options."[5]

More than 25 years after she completed her playing career, Miller is still recognized as an all-time great, even by players who never saw her shoot a ball. "I know her story," said Moore, who was the Naismith Award winner in 2009 while at the University of Connecticut and WNBA Rookie of the Year in 2011. Moore was born two years after Miller blew out her knee. "She was super-athletic," Moore said. "People marveled at her. She's got credibility—a legend of the game."[6]

Bringing Attention to Women's Basketball

Off the court is where Miller might have had her greatest impact. She played at a time when women's basketball was not on television much, and it didn't get a lot of coverage in the print media, either. Miller's overall game, including her dynamic personality, helped bring the sport into the national spotlight. She graced the cover of *Sports Illustrated*'s college basketball preview edition on November 20, 1985. In that edition, the magazine declared Miller as the best player in the country—male or female.

The 1984 Olympics in Los Angeles put Miller squarely in the spotlight. She put her greatness on display for the nation, and that opened some eyes to the sport of women's basketball. More than a decade after Miller stopped playing college basketball, the WNBA came into existence. The game made significant strides in those years, in large part because Miller brought attention to the sport. "You can really look back to Cheryl Miller as maybe not directly bringing about where basketball is today, but certainly indirectly and she was the first step," Callan said.[7]

When Miller was hired to coach the Phoenix Mercury in 1997, the WNBA's inaugural season, she might have been the biggest name in the league. She was certainly one of the most entertaining, despite being on the sidelines. Her name brought a pizzazz to the league. Miller's time as a WNBA coach and her years spent popularizing women's basketball have had at least an indirect impact on the continued success of the WNBA.

Miller's impact on the game is why she has been inducted into so many halls of fame over the years. She was a part of the inaugural class of the Women's Basketball Hall of Fame in 1999. She is also in the FIBA Hall of Fame, the International Women's Sports Hall of Fame, and the California Sports Hall of Fame. She also has a place in the grandest hall of them all, the Naismith Memorial Basketball Hall of Fame.

Cheryl and Reggie Make History

In 1995, Cheryl was inducted into the Naismith Memorial Basketball Hall of Fame in Springfield, Massachusetts. Years later, in 2012, her younger brother, Reggie Miller, was inducted into the same Hall of Fame. They became the first brother and sister to be inducted into the Hall of Fame. "This Miller family, it's not too shabby," Reggie said.[8]

"Reggie and Cheryl were such special competitors on the court," wrote ESPN college basketball analyst Dick Vitale in 2012. "It is great to see the siblings both will be in the shrine at Springfield. Cheryl shined in college at USC while Reggie excelled at UCLA. They attended rival schools but both were so special, so talented. The dynamic duo certainly brought a lot of pride and thrills to the Miller household."[9]

Was she the greatest ever? Miller will let others have that debate. As far as she is concerned, she simply played a game she loved and did it well. "I wasn't the greatest athlete and I couldn't jump out of the gym and I wasn't an extraordinary ball handler," she said. "I was just someone who loved the game so very much and had a passion for sport and life."[10]

Keeping Busy

When Miller is not working, she keeps herself busy in other ways. For years, she has been in high demand as a motivational speaker. She has also been a spokesperson for organizations such as the Los Angeles Literacy Campaign, the American Diabetes Association, the American Cancer Society, the American Lung Association, the Muscular Dystrophy Association, the African American Council for Big Sisters of Los Angeles, and the Pediatric Aids Foundation.

Cheryl and her brother Reggie Miller during his 2012 induction into the Naismith Memorial Basketball Hall of Fame

1964

Cheryl Miller is born on January 3, 1964, in Riverside, California.

1981

Miller averages 39.4 points and 16.3 rebounds per game as a junior at Riverside Polytechnic High School.

1982

As a high school senior, Miller scores 105 points in a game against Norte Vista.

1983

Miller helps the US team win a gold medal at the 1983 Pan American Games in Caracas, Venezuela.

1984

Miller scores 16 points in USC's 72–61 victory against Tennessee to win a second consecutive national title.

1984

Miller and Team USA defeat Spain to win the gold medal at the summer Olympics.

1982

Miller leads
Riverside Poly
to its first state
championship
and fourth
Southern Section
championship.

1982

Miller enters USC
as a freshman and
earns a spot in the
starting lineup
of the basketball
team.

1983

Miller scores
an NCAA
championship-game
record 27 points
in leading USC to
a 69–67 win over
Louisiana Tech for
the NCAA title.

1986

In her final game
at USC, Miller
scores 16 points
but fouls out in
the last quarter as
the Trojans lose to
Texas 97–81 in the
national title game.

1986

Miller leads
Team USA to
the FIBA World
Championship
gold medal with a
108–88 win over the
Soviet Union.

1987

During a pickup
game, Miller suffers
a serious injury
to her right knee,
leading to the
end of her playing
career.

1987

Miller begins her broadcasting career, working for ABC Sports and ESPN.

1987

Returning to USC, Miller accepts a position as an assistant coach.

1988

During tryouts for the Olympic team, Miller re-injures her knee and is released from the team.

1995

After two successful seasons, Miller resigns as USC's head coach for a job as a broadcast journalist with Turner Sports, covering the NBA.

1997

Miller becomes the head coach and general manager for the Phoenix Mercury of the newly formed WNBA.

1998

The Miller-led Mercury come up just short of winning the WNBA title, falling to the Houston Comets.

1992

After being named one of 18 finalists for the Olympic team, Miller gives up her spot due to ongoing knee trouble.

1993

Miller accepts an offer to become head coach at USC.

1995

Miller is enshrined in the Naismith Basketball Hall of Fame.

1999

Miller is a part of the inaugural class of the Women's Basketball Hall of Fame in Knoxville, Tennessee.

2000

After four seasons, Miller resigns as head coach of the Mercury.

2012

Reggie and Cheryl become the first brother and sister to be enshrined in the Naismith Basketball Hall of Fame.

ESSENTIAL FACTS

DATE OF BIRTH

January 3, 1964

PLACE OF BIRTH

Riverside, California

PARENTS

Saul and Carrie Miller

EDUCATION

Riverside Polytechnic High School (1978–1982)

University of Southern California (1982–1986)

CAREER HIGHLIGHTS

Cheryl Miller was the only women's basketball player to earn high school All-American honors four times and college All-American honors four times. She led her high school team to four consecutive section championships and then won back-to-back national titles at USC in 1983 and 1984. In 1984, Miller contributed to Team USA's gold medal win at the Olympics. Miller has had success in coaching and broadcasting, as well.

SOCIAL CONTRIBUTIONS

With exceptional ability and an outgoing personality, Miller was the first true superstar in women's basketball. She helped bring the game into a brighter spotlight. Over the years, she has also been a motivational speaker and a spokesperson for organizations such as the Los Angeles Literacy Campaign, the American Diabetes Association, the American Cancer Society, the American Lung Association, the Muscular Dystrophy Association, the African American Council for Big Sisters of Los Angeles, and the Pediatric Aids Foundation.

CONFLICTS

Some people criticized the way Miller played the game, citing too much showmanship and arrogance. She faced controversy when she accepted the head coaching position at USC for not backing the previous head coach's fight for pay equal to that of the men's basketball coach. Additionally, she was criticized for letting her broadcasting career interfere with coaching when she was head coach of the Phoenix Mercury.

QUOTE

"I wasn't the greatest athlete and I couldn't jump out of the gym and I wasn't an extraordinary ball handler. I was just someone who loved the game so very much and had a passion for sport and life."—*Cheryl Miller*

GLOSSARY

All-American

A player named as one of the best high school or college players in the United States.

assist

A pass to a teammate that directly leads to a basket.

boycott

To refuse something in protest.

cultivate

To work on something over time, to help it grow.

draft

A system in sports in which each team in a league selects an incoming player. The order of picks is generally determined by the regular-season record, with the worst teams picking first.

dunk

When a basketball player scores in a game by slamming the ball through the hoop.

foul

An infraction called for illegal personal contact or unsportsmanlike conduct.

free throw

A shot in basketball that a player takes after being fouled.

full-court press

A defense used when one team tries to stop another all the way down the court.

hustle

To hide one's talent before making a bet, only to reveal that talent in winning the bet.

induct
  To admit as a member.

layup
  In basketball, a one-handed shot taken close to the hoop, typically using the backboard.

playoff
  A series of games played after the regular season by the best teams in a league in order to determine a champion.

prestigious
  Having a high reputation.

rebound
  Gaining possession of the basketball after a failed shot.

recruit
  To try to get players from a lower level, such as high school, to play for a higher level, such as college.

revolutionize
  To change completely.

scholarship
  Money awarded to a student to help pay for school. Great athletes are sometimes given athletic scholarships in order to represent a school through its sports teams.

showmanship
  The presentation of something in a theatrical way.

sportsmanship
  The conduct becoming to one participating in a sport.

zone defense
  A defense used in basketball in which players on a team cover a specific area rather than guarding a specific player.

SELECTED BIBLIOGRAPHY

Johnson, Anne Janette. *Great Women in Sports*. Detroit, MI: Visible Ink Press, 1996. Print.

Weeks, Matthew James. "A Game of the Century Mark." *USA Today*. USA Today, 1 Feb. 2001. Web. 6 Sept. 2013.

Woolum, Janet. *Outstanding Women Athletes: Who They Are and How They Influenced Sports in America*. Phoenix, AZ: Oryx Press, 1992. Print.

FURTHER READINGS

Baker, Christine A. *Why She Plays: The World of Women's Basketball*. Lincoln, NE: University of Nebraska Press, 2008. Print.

Grundy, Pamela, and Susan Shackelford. *Shattering the Glass: The Remarkable History of Women's Basketball*. New York: New Press, 2005. Print.

Lieberman, Nancy. *Basketball for Women*. Champaign, IL: Human Kinetics, 2012. Print.

WEB LINKS

To learn more about Cheryl Miller, visit ABDO Publishing Company online at **www.abdopublishing.com**. Web sites about Cheryl Miller are featured on our Book Links page. These links are routinely monitored and updated to provide the most current information available.

PLACES TO VISIT

Galen Center
University of Southern California
3400 South Figueroa Street, Los Angeles, CA 90007
213-740-0626
www.usctrojans.com/facilities/usc-galen-center.html
The Galen Center is home to the USC Trojans basketball teams.

Naismith Memorial Basketball Hall of Fame
1000 Hall of Fame Avenue, Springfield, MA 01105
413-781-6500
www.hoophall.com
The basketball hall of fame details basketball's history and key events. The 40,000-square-foot space hosts numerous exhibits detailing the sport's inductees, including Miller.

Women's Basketball Hall of Fame
700 Hall of Fame Drive, Knoxville, TN 37915
865-633-9000
www.wbhof.com
The Women's Basketball Hall of Fame preserves the history of women's basketball and includes inductees who have impacted the sport, such as Miller.

SOURCE NOTES

CHAPTER 1. 105 Points

1. Matthew James Weeks. "A Game of the Century Mark." *USA Today*. USA Today, 1 Feb. 2001. Web. 6 Sept. 2013.
2. Ibid.
3. Ibid.
4. Ibid.
5. Gregg Patton. "Riverside: Miller's 105-Point Game No. 1 Unbreakable Record." *Press-Enterprise*. Enterprise Media, 11 July 2011. Web. 6 Sept. 2013.
6. Ibid.
7. Matthew James Weeks. "A Game of the Century Mark." *USA Today*. USA Today, 1 Feb. 2001. Web. 6 Sept. 2013.

CHAPTER 2. Childhood

1. Official Hoop Hall. "Cheryl Miller's Basketball Hall of Fame Enshrinement Speech." Online video clip. *YouTube*. Google, 29 June 2012. Web. 9 Sept. 2013.
2. Kevin Cook. "Team Miller: Plenty of Discipline, a Basketball Hoop in the Driveway and Oatmeal Every Morning—That's the Millers' Recipe for Success." *Los Angeles Times*. Los Angeles Times, 6 Oct. 1991. Web. 6 Sept. 2013.
3. Curry Kirkpatrick. "Lights! Camera! Cheryl!" *SI Vault*. Time Inc., 20 Nov. 1985. Web. 6 Sept. 2013.
4. Ibid.
5. Ibid.
6. Kevin Cook. "Team Miller: Plenty of Discipline, a Basketball Hoop in the Driveway and Oatmeal Every Morning—That's the Millers' Recipe for Success." *Los Angeles Times*. Los Angeles Times, 6 Oct. 1991. Web. 6 Sept. 2013.
7. Ibid.
8. Janet Woolum. *Outstanding Women Athletes: Who They Are and How They Influenced Sports in America*. Phoenix, AZ: Oryx Press, 1992. Print. 154.
9. Kurt Helin. "How Reggie, Cheryl Miller Used to Hustle Playground Games." *NBC Sports*. NBC Sports, 7 Sept. 2012. Web. 6 Sept. 2013.
10. Official Hoop Hall. Reggie Miller's Basketball Hall of Fame Enshrinement Speech. Online video clip. *YouTube*. Google, 9 Sept. 2012. Web. 6 Sept. 2013.

CHAPTER 3. High School Days

1. Roger Jackson. "She May Well Be the Best Ever." *SI Vault*. Time Inc., 29 Nov. 1982. Web. 6 Sept. 2013.

2. Ibid.

3. Ibid.

4. Matthew James Weeks. "A Game of the Century Mark." *USA Today*. USA Today, 1 Feb. 2001. Web. 6 Sept. 2013.

5. Gregg Patton. "Riverside: Miller's 105-Point Game No. 1 Unbreakable Record." *Press-Enterprise*. Enterprise Media, 11 July 2011. Web. 6 Sept. 2013.

6. Matthew James Weeks. "A Game of the Century Mark." *USA Today*. USA Today, 1 Feb. 2001. Web. 6 Sept. 2013.

7. Roger Jackson. "She May Well Be the Best Ever." *SI Vault*. Time Inc., 29 Nov. 1982. Web. 6 Sept. 2013.

8. Gordon S. White Jr. "Schoolgirl Is Reaching Heights." *New York Times*. New York Times Company, 3 Feb. 1982. Web. 6 Sept. 2013.

CHAPTER 4. College Hoops

1. Roger Jackson. "She May Well Be the Best Ever." *SI Vault*. Time Inc., 29 Nov. 1982. Web. 6 Sept. 2013.

2. Ibid.

3. Ibid.

4. Ibid.

5. Ibid.

6. Jill Lieber. "Stars of Stage, Screen and Court." *SI Vault*. Time Inc., 9 Apr. 1984. Web. 6 Sept. 2013.

7. Curry Kirkpatrick. "Lights! Camera! Cheryl!" *SI Vault*. Time Inc., 20 Nov. 1985. Web. 6 Sept. 2013.

8. Kevin Cook. "Team Miller: Plenty of Discipline, a Basketball Hoop in the Driveway and Oatmeal Every Morning—That's the Millers' Recipe for Success." *Los Angeles Times*. Los Angeles Times, 6 Oct. 1991. Web. 6 Sept. 2013.

9. Carol Callan. Personal interview. 11 June 2013.

CHAPTER 5. Team USA

1. "USC's Cheryl Miller Living Up to High School Rave Notices So Far." *Christian Science Monitor*. Christian Science Monitor, n.d. Web. 6 Sept. 2013.

2. Ibid.

3. Malcolm Moran. "Triumph and Defeat for American Women; South Korea Trounced." *New York Times*. New York Times Company, 8 Aug. 1984. Web. 6 Sept. 2013.

CHAPTER 6. Nowhere to Play

1. Carol Callan. Personal interview. 11 June 2013.

2. Curry Kirkpatrick. "Lights! Camera! Cheryl!" *SI Vault*. Time Inc., 20 Nov. 1985. Web. 6 Sept. 2013.

3. Kevin Cook. "Team Miller: Plenty of Discipline, a Basketball Hoop in the Driveway and Oatmeal Every Morning—That's the Millers' Recipe for Success." *Los Angeles Times*. Los Angeles Times, 6 Oct. 1991. Web. 6 Sept. 2013.

4. Mel Greenberg. "Miller Is Dropped from the Women's Basketball Team." *Philadelphia Inquirer*. Philadelphia Media Network, 10 Aug. 1988. Web. 6 Sept. 2013.

5. Julie Cart. "Cheryl Miller: Sure, She's a Hotdog; Sure, She's Hollywood—but She's Herself." *Los Angeles Times*. Los Angeles Times, 2 Mar. 1986. Web. 6 Sept. 2013.

6. "Interview of the Week: FIBA Hall of Famer Cheryl Miller." *Heinnews*. Heinnews, n.d. Web. 6 Sept. 2013.

CHAPTER 7. Coach Miller

1. "USC Nets Cheryl Miller." *USC News*. University of Southern California, 13 Sept. 1993. Web. 6 Sept. 2013.

2. Richard Hoffer. "Cheryl Miller." *SI Vault*. Time Inc., 6 Dec. 1993. Web. 6 Sept. 2013.

3. Jerry Brewer. "Miller Sets Fans, Foes to Talking." *Philadelphia Inquirer*. Philadelphia Media Network, 17 July 2000. Web. 6 Sept. 2013.

4. Richard Hoffer. "Cheryl Miller." *SI Vault*. Time Inc., 6 Dec. 1993. Web. 6 Sept. 2013.

5. Ibid.

6. Associated Press. "Mercury Coach Cheryl Miller Resigns." *AP News Archive*. Associated Press, 1 Dec. 2000. Web. 6 Sept. 2013.

7. Earl Gustkey. "Cheryl Miller Resigns as USC Coach." *Los Angeles Times*. Los Angeles Times, 16 Sept. 1995. Web. 6 Sept. 2013.

8. Carol Callan. Personal interview. 11 June 2013.

9. Associated Press. "Mercury Coach Cheryl Miller Resigns." *AP News Archive*. Associated Press, 1 Dec. 2000. Web. 6 Sept. 2013.

CHAPTER 8. Miller on Television

1. Berry Tramel. "Q&A with TNT Reporter Cheryl Miller." *NewsOK*. NewsOK.com, 22 May 2011. Web. 6 Sept. 2013.

2. Carol Callan. Personal interview. 11 June 2013.

3. Julie Cart. "Cheryl Miller: Sure, She's a Hotdog; Sure, She's Hollywood—but She's Herself." *Los Angeles Times*. Los Angeles Times, 2 Mar. 1986. Web. 6 Sept. 2013.

4. Gordon S. White Jr. "Schoolgirl Is Reaching Heights." *New York Times*. New York Times Company, 3 Feb. 1982. Web. 6 Sept. 2013.

5. Mike Trudell. "Cheryl Miller Talks Hoops." *WNBA.com*. WNBA Enterprises, n.d. Web. 6 Sept. 2013.

6. Ibid.

CHAPTER 9. Ongoing Legacy

1. Carol Callan. Personal interview. 11 June 2013.

2. Anne Janette Johnson. *Great Women in Sports*. Detroit, MI: Visible Ink Press, 1996. Print. 338.

3. Curry Kirkpatrick. "Lights! Camera! Cheryl!" *SI Vault*. Time Inc., 20 Nov. 1985. Web. 6 Sept. 2013.

4. Ibid.

5. Carol Callan. Personal interview. 11 June 2013.

6. "40 Greatest Female Athletes: Cheryl Miller." *ESPN*. ESPN.com, 6 June 2012. Web. 6 Sept. 2013.

7. Carol Callan. Personal interview. 11 June 2013.

8. Jeff Zillgitt. "Reggie Miller Can't Wait to Join Sister in Hall of Fame." *USA Today*. USA Today, 3 Sept. 2012. 6 Sept. 2013.

9. Dick Vitale. "It's Miller Time in Springfield." *ESPN*. ESPN.com, 8 Sept. 2012. 6 Sept. 2013.

10. Anne Janette Johnson. *Great Women in Sports*. Detroit, MI: Visible Ink Press, 1996. Print. 341.

ABOUT THE AUTHOR

Brian Howell is a freelance writer based in Denver, Colorado. He has been a sports journalist for nearly 20 years, writing about high school, college, and professional athletics. In addition, he has written books about sports and history. He lives with his wife and four children.

PHOTO CREDITS

TSN/Icon SMI/Newscom, cover, 3, 27, 96 (top); Jon Soohoo/ Bettmann/Corbis, 6; Ray Stubblebine/AP Images, 13, 22, 51, 97 (top left), 97 (bottom); Dave Tenenbaum/AP Images, 14, 46; Joseph S. L. Tan Matt/Shutterstock Images, 21; G.F. Bryant/ AP Images, 31; Alvin Chung/AP Images, 32; Reed Saxon/AP Images, 35, 97 (top right); Lennox McLendon/AP Images, 38; Bettmann/Corbis, 40; Nick Ut/AP Images, 45, 96 (bottom); Wally McNamee/Corbis, 53; AP Images, 55; Bob Bryant/AP Images, 56; Jessica Hill/AP Images, 59; 2010 Kathy Hutchins/ Hutchins Photo/Newscom, 61; Tim Clayton/Corbis, 63; Daniel Anderson/KLT/Newscom, 65; Matt York/AP Images, 66; Splash News/Corbis, 69, 99 (top); Jason Wise/AP Images, 71; Scott Troyanos/AP Images, 75; Icon Sports Media, 76, 98 (top); Kevin Reece/Icon SMI, 80; Tom Strattman/AP Images, 83; Shutterstock Images, 84; Francis Specker/AP Images, 87, 99 (bottom left); Roy Dabner/AP Images, 88, 98 (bottom); Matt A. Brown/Icon SMI, 90; Elise Amendola/AP Images, 95, 99 (bottom right)